GRANDFATHER TALES

AND OTHER STORIES OF SMALL TOWN LIFE

Hal Duvall

DEDICATION

This book of stories and recollections is dedicated to my grandchildren. In chronological order

Belinthia

Will

Jackson

Charlie

Crawford

and Sallie

I hope I turn out to be as much fun for them as Na Na was for me.

ACKNOWLEDGEMENTS

I'd like to thank Patricia Barnes, Bob Whiteman, and Anne and Frank Watson for helping me with pathfinding and direction, keyboarding, and other gritty little details involved in getting words on paper using a computer. They are both friends and scenery.

GRANDFATHER TALES

AND OTHER STORIES OF SMALL TOWN LIFE

Hal Duvall

My grandfather enjoyed life. He loved getting together with friends to share a meal, a drink, a game of cards, or a few hours in a fishing boat. He would often get a small group together and drive to Myrtle Beach or a fishing spot in Florida. Those two venues offered the opportunity to give cards *and* fishing the attention each deserved.

Myrtle Beach was more accessible from Cheraw, so the group often loaded into a car or two and crossed the river heading east. A funny thing happened to the individuals when the expedition crossed the river: The dignified and upright bankers, businessmen, doctors, and lawyers underwent a transformation. They became boys on holiday. For example, the man known in Cheraw as "that sweet little Mr. ABC" was known to most of the waitresses in Myrtle Beach as "the wildcat."

Myrtle Beach in the early thirties was a far different place than it is today. The roads were deep sandy ruts. There were no hotels and few houses. It was said you could buy all the beach-front property you wanted for five dollars an acre, if you had the five dollars. Times were hard, but these men left their businesses and got away for a little. They knew they had more time than money!

They usually stayed (and ate) at one of the boarding houses on the beach. They rotated through the responsibility for calling ahead (long distance!) and making reservations for the group. Once when it was my grandfather's turn to make the arrangements, He was astonished when they arrived and were told there were no rooms for H. P. Duvall. He asked to see the list of reservations, and sure enough, there several rooms reserved for H. Peter Ball! He was called "Pete" all that weekend, and some of the bunch called him Pete until the day he died.

On another occasion, the car pulled up at another boarding house, and one of the men went inside to announce their arrival. He soon reappeared with his arm around one of the sisters who ran the place, and the two of them came out to the car. In a few minutes a second sister appeared, and his arm went around her also. When a third woman emerged from the house, my grandfather's friend Ernest leaned over to him in the back seat. In a stage whisper he asked, "Hal, what in the hell is 'Biggety' going to do now?"

My grandfather also loved to play games with his grandchildren. When I was four or five, a swing set was set up in our side yard. When my grandfather came home that evening, he insisted on "skinning the cat"—in his mid-fifties!—before going inside.

There were times when several grandchildren were present, and my grandfather would sometimes join their games. He would sit on his front steps facing the sidewalk while the children lined up on the sidewalk and faced him. He called out instructions: "Howard, take two giant steps." If Howard remembered to ask, "Mother, may I?" he was allowed to move forward. My grandfather continued, giving instructions to each child in turn, doing his best to keep the game close and fun, until one of us made it to the steps where he sat.

My grandfather received his education in the Cheraw School, which educated students to the sixth grade, and was not free. After six grades, few students received further schooling. Because he enjoyed reading, my grandfather was a fairly well- educated man. When his younger son, Teddy, was in high school, my grandfather asked what they had talked about in history that day. Teddy told him that they had been learning about "Napoleon," was the answer. "Who's that?" asked my grandfather. "Oh, Dad, you know—the Emperor of the French." My grandfather responded, "Oh, you mean Nap-o-*le*-on!" He knew the man from his reading, but had never heard his name pronounced!

As a young man, my grandfather joined the hardware business owned by his father and older brother, Walker. He soon married Rena Wannamaker, and pretty soon they had three boys: Hal, Howard ("Hiney"), and Teddy. When my father, Hal, was born, my grandfather reported to Walker when he got to work, "Me and Dr. Bull had us a baby boy about four o'clock this morning."

The brothers got along very well together, though they were active boys and far from angels .My grandfather was frequently seen pedaling his bicycle furiously down Powe Street toward home, removing his belt as he rode to settle some argument.

Rena was not a healthy person, and she died in 1918. This left my grandfather a widower at age forty with three active boys. A succession of female family members moved into the house on Greene Street to serve as housekeeper. This lasted until 1931 when my parents moved back to Cheraw. Daddy joined the family hardware business and Mother inherited the position of housekeeper in a house full of men—her husband and six-month-old son, a father-in-law, and two brothers-in-law. Up to that point Mother had never kept house. She had a good bit of domestic help on Greene Street and we got along.

NA NA AND
THE CAPTAIN

I called my grandfather "Na Na" (pronounced like the sound a sheep makes—not like the last two syllables of *banana,* which, to my mind, is reserved for grandmothers). He called me "Captain." We were buddies. We were even on the same schedule. Na Na usually went to bed right after supper, often taking a cold biscuit and a little piece of cheese with him. He woke at first light. His buddy the Captain was also put to bed right after supper (with a sigh of relief from my mother), and I, too, was awake at first light.

When I was released from bed, I headed up the hall to Na Na's room and crawled into bed with him. Sometimes we would have conversations and sometimes he would tell me stories. Mother said he made up many of the stories, but when I was older he would tell me his version of one of the classic stories from *Arabian Nights*, like "Sinbad the Sailor," "Ali Baba and the Forty Thieves," and "Aladdin and His Wonderful Lamp." I recently realized I had never actually read those stories, so I went to the library and checked out a copy.

Let me tell you one thing—my Na Na was a masterful storyteller if he could tell those stories to a preschooler without scaring him to death! They are *terrible* stories about murder, blood, deceit, magic, and trickery. I could not even finish the book, but I absolutely loved it as a child when Na Na told me his versions.

I can see him now, sitting at the head of the table in the dining room, head bowed, thanking the Lord for what we were "battery-ceive." At least that's what "about to receive" sounded like to me. My uncle Hiney "battery-ceived" all his life. He was a lot like Na Na.

Na Na loved breakfast bacon, which he called "breakfast strip." He held it delicately between two fingers, pinkie finger raised like a lady drinking tea, and admired it for a moment before taking a bite. He also loved salt mackerel, and there was often a little wooden cask of it on the floor in the kitchen. If he was offered ice cream for dessert, he would ask, "Do you have any of those little cakes?" (He always called cookies "cakes.") Also he was addicted to White Owl five-cent cigars.

He spanked me only once—the first time I ever mistook an order for a suggestion. He did not hesitate, and I learned a good lesson. Don't mess with Na Na!

Na Na, as I said earlier, lost his wife when he was forty. I never heard that he showed any interest in a long-term (or even a short-term) relationship with a woman after his wife died. He liked women and liked to talk with them, but anything closer than arm's length was too close for him. Most of the women he paid attention to or gave gifts to were women who worked in the stores and offices downtown. Several mornings each week he would visit the grocery stores and drugstores, pick up some fruit or small boxes of candy, and distribute them to his girlfriends. Deliveries made, he returned to his hardware store, opened the cash register, and withdrew the money for his purchases. A clerk would be sent with the money to pay the bills he had made fifteen minutes before.

He did have one special lady friend. Miss Nan moved here in 1920 as a bride. She and her husband invited my grandfather, a recent widower, to join them on Sunday afternoon drives and picnics. Twenty years later when

Nan's husband died, Na Na had no thought of elevating the relationship. "An arm's length" friendship was his aim. Romance was not.

When Na Na's middle son, Hiney, was in high school he had a crush on a girl. One day he asked his father, "Daddy, does your heart go pitty-pat when you see Miss Nan like mine does when I see Marg?"

Na Na's feet hurt. He had corns, and shoes were not comfortable. When he bought a new pair, he brought them back to the hardware store and directed one of the men to take his pocketknife and cut slits in the new shoes to relieve the pressure on his corns.

The Carolina army maneuvers took place around Cheraw for several weeks in

September and October of 1941. Thousands of soldiers were bivouacked in the countryside. The maneuvers took place Monday through Friday, so most soldiers had three-day passes and headed to a nearby town. The Red Cross asked citizens to offer their extra bedrooms to soldiers while they were in town. Many did this—we did at our house, and Hiney did at his. (Imagine that today!)

Fifty years later, one of those soldiers who had stayed weekends at Hiney's house came to the store looking for Mr. Duvall. He was traveling through the South, showing his wife and daughter where he had been. One of his memories was of pitching pennies at a crack in the floor with the "old man."

During the maneuvers, the Red Cross also sponsored dances for the soldiers during the weekend. There were not enough single women to go around, so the Red Cross appealed to married couples: "Husbands, please bring your wives to the dances and let them dance with the soldiers while you sit on the sidelines." My mother loved to dance, and Daddy sat on the sidelines while she enjoyed herself. She had regular partners for certain dances, like her "polka boy" and her "waltz boy."

In the late forties, Na Na began having trouble with high blood pressure and his health declined. One evening in November 1952, he finished his supper, picked up a cold biscuit and a little piece of cheese like usual, and retired to his room. He did not show up for breakfast the next morning and Hiney found him on the floor, still clothed from the evening before, the biscuit and cheese uneaten.

NA NA'S LETTERS

Here are two letters Na Na wrote me when I was six and seven. Notice the casual address on the envelopes, yet they were delivered by the post office! The Charles referred to in the first letter is my brother. He was fourteen months old at this time. I'm grateful to Mother for saving these, addressed to:

Captain Hal Duvall

Cheraw, SC

They were written in pencil on hotel stationery from

The Island Inn

Sanibel Island, Florida

In the Gulf of Mexico

Jan. 12, 1937
Monday night

Dear Captain,

This is Na Na writing just after sup-per. Boy, have we been catching the fish! Any about the size of Charles I throw back in the water as being too small to worry with, but when I get one your size I save him for the fry pan.

I want to tell you about the nicest fish I lost today, and how I lost him. I had been fishing for three or four minutes and hadn't had a bite, and I was getting ready to quit and come in—when something yanked my line and I pulled out a beauty. It was just your size and had ears like yours. I was sure pleased, and just as I started to put him in my hip pocket, he said, "Pardon me, but aren't you Mr. Duvall?" You can imagine how surprised I was. I said, "How do you know my name?" He said, "My father and mother have told me many times about a fine handsome man named Mr. Duvall that was down here some years ago. When I looked at you, I knew you at once."

I was surprised again, and I said, "Well, little scalawag, since you speak so nicely about me, I will throw you back in the water."

So I took him between my thumb and little finger and threw him way out in the ocean. Just before he hit the water he made a flip and hollered back, "Ha! Ha! Fooled you that time! I never knew you before!" And that is how I lost him.

I will tell you some more true stories when I get home. Love from Guess Who

The second letter is written on the same type stationery and the same casual address for me. It is postmarked Jan 17, 1938.

Well, Captain, here I am again at the tropical island of Sanibel, Florida, USA.

Bud, it always pays to be kind to dumb animals. I want you to remember this, and I will tell you of an adventure I had today that will show you what I mean. On a tropical island everything grows very fast, so you will understand my adventure today.

Adventure Of H. P. Duvall
On The Gulf Of Mexico
This 16Th Day Of January, 1938

We were fishing the placid waters of the Gulf of Mexico today, and I was rapidly filling up the fish box with all manner of nice fish. My son Hiney had landed a few small ones, much to his pleasure.

Suddenly the Captain gave a cry of "Save yourselves! Every man for himself!" and he dived in the bottom of the boat and commenced to put on all the life belts. Hiney fainted, and the girls commenced to pull their dresses down over their knees (to keep from getting bit on the legs).

When I looked up to ascertain the cause of all the alarm I saw a monster fish approaching the boat at lightning speed. The danger was terrible, but I decided to face it coolly, and raised my hand to continue smoking, when I found I had swallowed my cigar. I smoothed my hair, stuck out my chest, and faced the danger like a man. I suddenly smelled an odor that I first thought was my cigar, burning up my insides, but was relieved to find that it was caused by the large fish putting on brakes too fast as he approached our boat, scorching the water around him.

Now comes the strangest part of the story, for as I looked into his face I suddenly saw it was the little scalawag I had thrown back in the ocean last year, and that he was smiling at me. Before I knew what to do, he stood up on his tail in the water, and kissed me smack in the mouth!

I felt like I ought to do something in return, so I thought quickly (as I always do) that I should give him something useful to remember me by. As I thought about how wet the water was, I jumped up and threw him my raincoat that I was sitting on. He swam slowly to it until it fitted snugly around his shoulders, and then, smiling broadly, he swam away. And while he did not say a word, I knew he was thinking, "that Mr. Duvall is a nice man."

Now, you see, Bud, if I had not been nice to him last year and he had swallowed me up, I would have had a painful experience instead of a pleasant adventure. So, always be kind to dumb animals.

You may doubt some of this story, so I wish when we get home Hiney could tell you about it, but unluckily he was fainted all the time in the bottom of the boat.

Love to you and Charles and your Pa and Ma.

Na Na

BASEBALL TALES

Cheraw has always been a baseball town. Around the turn of the twentieth century, it boasted an excellent amateur team that competed against nearby (and not-so-nearby) towns. In those days the roads weren't dependable, so the teams traveled by train.

The black citizens of Cheraw were interested in baseball too. James, a catcher, wore a sweatshirt with THOU SHALT NOT STEAL written in big, bold letters on the back.

Before the time of radio or television, the baseball fans of Cheraw were able to listen to the World Series by gathering at the town hall, where Western Union received, by wire, a report of each pitch. Someone was designated to announce the action to the assembled crowd: "The count is two and two, with one out!"

In the thirties there was a Cheraw team in the Sandhill League in which some players received money to play. "Bobo" Newsom from Hartsville played for the Cheraw team until he was traded to another team for two bats and three balls! Bobo was quite a clown and a party boy who later pitched for the Detroit Tigers in the 1940 World Series when they were beaten by the Cincinnati Reds. Van Mungo of Pageland, later a fastball pitcher for the Dodgers, was also in the league.

In the early days, a horse-drawn wagon would drive through the streets with a big sign that said BASEBALL TODAY. Games were also publicized by word of mouth. I can remember seeing a slow-moving automobile driving through the town. In the back seat a man with a megaphone called out, "Baseball this afternoon at four o'clock. Cheraw versus Pageland." A few hundred people would show up to most games. There wasn't much else to do.

Hiney told me that business was awful slow in the early thirties. If he had to leave the store to make a delivery, he would swing by the baseball field and watch a couple of innings before going back to work. Often, no one would have moved while he was gone!

Many fans used empty Coke bottles to beat against the grandstand's metal roof or wooden seats to stir up noise for a rally. Jack Poston and Thornton Malloy seldom missed a game. If the opposing team got a man on base, Jack could be counted on to bellow out in his foghorn voice, "Out'en 'em!"

HAL DUVALL

In the last days of World War II, coaches were very hard to come by—practically every man who could walk was in the service. Jack was asked to coach the high school team during this time. It turned out to be one of the better teams in the history of the school, and it advanced to the semifinals for the state championship.

The team was notable for more than the quality of its play. The infielders averaged little more than 100 pounds each. Miller Ingram, who played first base, weighed 110. The second baseman, Breeden Laney, was the "big guy" at 122. The shortstop, J. L. "Jap" Spears, was only 92 pounds. The seventh grader at third base, Austin "Tom" Brewer, weighed 100. The latter two played professional ball in later years. Spears was with the Dodger organization's Triple-A team for several years. "Pee Wee" Reese, the Dodger shortstop, kept Spears at Triple-A level.

Tom Brewer pitched eight seasons for the Boston Red Sox in the major leagues, beginning in 1954. In his third season his record was 19–9, and he pitched in the All-Star Game. Even in his retirement he works every spring with countless young pitchers who want to learn the game.

Some of our fans are die-hards. It is said that one man in our town has a complete set of New York Yankee pinstripes in his closet. When the Yankees are playing in the World Series, he wears his pinstripes and watches them on television at home.

According to town legend, one year he prepared to enjoy the game by himself. He locked the doors, took the phone off the hook so he wouldn't be disturbed, and turned on the television. It was an exciting, tight game. Then, in the middle of the fifth inning his doorbell began to ring insistently. Grumbling mightily, he made his way to the door and opened it. There were two handsome women, hatted and gloved, waiting there with expectant expressions. They asked, by name, for the man who had answered the door, explaining that they had found him *so* charming at the university twenty years before. "Does he still live here?" they asked. The baseball fan said, "No, he died." He closed and locked the door as he hurried back to the game.

Cheraw was filled with excitement in the mid-1950s when the first Little League teams were organized here. The boys wore their uniforms everywhere—whether there was a game or not. The coaches kept their competitive instinct at a low level, concentrating on teaching the rudiments of the game as well as good sportsmanship.

Games were scheduled three afternoons a week after the workday was over. The stands were filled with parents and siblings of players, and many others who simply enjoyed watching the young folks play. The cheering was vigorous and good-natured.

One day a batter was at the plate, waiting for the pitch. He was a rawboned eleven-year-old with a strong build and a prominent nose. "Hit it with your nose, Sam!" yelled someone in the stands.

There were a few chuckles.

Sam's mother, sitting a few rows in front, stood up and turned around, hands on hips, in mock anger.

"Who said that?" she demanded. Then she grinned.

WAR TALES

During World War II, many young boys entered the service as soon as they finished high school. Some secured their family's permission to enlist before finishing high school. Some even falsified documents so they could enlist without their family's permission. It was a time of high patriotism, the highest level of patriotism this country has ever seen. Here is the tale of one who entered the Navy with his parents' permission, told in his own words as well as I remember them.

"When I was sixteen I quit school and joined the Navy. Didn't like school much, and most of my friends was already in the service— the war had been going on two or three years. When I finished basic, the Navy put me on a small ship stationed in Florida, and we were used as a training ship for officers. I thought it was mighty strange—me, practically a high school dropout, just barely finished basic, and we was a training ship for *officers*!

"Well, one day we was out, and a young officer from Texas was on the bridge. He called down to where I was: '"Jones, what's our heading?' 'Three hundred fifty degrees, sir,' I answered. After a few minutes he called back: 'Change course to three hundred seventy-nine degrees.' 'Can't do that, sir. The compass only has three hundred sixty degrees on it' Then I heard him as he turned away, '*Damn* small boats, anyhow!'"

Robert was a Marine, fighting for his life on Iwo Jima. His high school buddy Will was on a Navy ship that was part of the flotilla in support of that engagement. Thankfully, both men made it through the war and returned to Cheraw. When they saw each other for the first time after the war, Will pretended to be upset with Robert.

"Don't want to have anything to do with you!" he said. "You high-hatted me, out there on Iwo!" "How could I have done that? Don't remember seeing you." "Well, you did. My ship went around that island three times. I waved all three times, and you never waved back!"

When Ed was in high school, he made what he thought was a wise decision. Short of money, as we all were in high school, he took advantage of an opportunity to join the National Guard, drill one weekend a month, and bring in some serious money. And the plan worked.

They paid him well and did not interfere in his life very much.

Then the National Guard was activated in 1950 and Ed found himself in Minnesota and later in Korea. Not too long after that he received a Dear John from the girl he had been dating back home. "She told me she didn't love me anymore, and then she sent me the name and address of a girl she thought I might like! I was upset and when I got to a place I could be alone, I took it to God in prayer."

"I said, 'God, is this a person you'd like for me to know?'

"And He said, 'This is the person I've been trying to get you with all along.'

"After another year in Korea, the army sent me home again. I went to see the girl whose address had been sent. I presented her with a diamond and told her the story. I said, 'This diamond is not just from me. It's from God, too!' She accepted me on that basis, and we have been married for forty years."

The famous Civil War general "Stonewall" Jackson was wounded at the battle of Chancellorsville and died a week later on May 10, 1863. His death was a terrible blow to the South, both psychologically and militarily. The war finally ended, leaving the South destitute. Twenty percent of its men were dead on the battlefield, and an equal number of grieving, resolute women were left behind.

In the early days of Reconstruction, the women of Cheraw somehow raised enough money to commission an eight-foot-tall white marble column. It was erected in St. David's Cemetery on July 26, 1867, only two years after the war ended. It was the first monument ever erected to the fallen Confederate soldiers.

In the years that followed, May 10 was recognized in Southern states as Confederate Memorial Day, as separate from the May 30 Memorial Day recognized by the rest of the nation. (That separation is finally ending.)

Cheraw developed its own tradition for the Tenth of May. Here's how it went: First and foremost, a parade was led by the surviving veterans of the Confederate Army in their tattered uniforms, carrying their flags. The parade ended at the monument in St. David's Cemetery. Bystanders gathered, filed through the enclosure, scattered flowers on the ground, and sang Civil War songs like "Tenting Tonight" and "Let Us Cross over the River and Rest under the Shade of the Trees," said to be Stonewall's last words. Then a prominent person gave a speech recalling the Lost Cause.

In later years, there were no more veterans in uniform, so school children were invited to march. On the Sunday afternoon nearest the tenth of May, the parade formed at the school on Greene Street. Children in their "Sunday best" were formed into line by teachers. The parade moved toward the Cemetery via Market and Second Streets, finally arriving at the monument and strewing their flowers on the ground before encircling the enclosure for songs and speeches. To encourage participation, each child who marched on Sunday was released from school two hours early on Monday.

Most children were allowed to go barefoot after theTenth and to remove the long underwear they had worn all winter. At the hardware store, we were allowed to take down the potbellied cast-iron heater that had been our only source of heat through the cold months.

At a Tenth of May parade in a small Southern town like Cheraw, a visitor watched the lines of gray-clad men as they marched stiffly and proudly to the beat of a drum. Each was consciously ramrod straight, chest out, face serious. Just as the observer was admiring the pride and discipline of these marchers he was distracted by something—something not quite right. In the last file of the marching men was a curious figure, clothed like the others in a gray uniform; yet his feet and legs were gyrating wildly as he attempted to keep pace with the drum. It was bizarre and almost comical. As he turned away from the parade, the visitor asked a town resident about the unusual marcher. "Oh, that's Sam," he said. "He was one of the first to volunteer in 1861. Marched off to Virginia in great excitement, eager to help the cause. In his first engagement, he was overcome by fear and ran wildly to the rear. When he was caught, he was punished for running in a way armies have used before. They cut his Achilles tendon behind both ankles to ensure he would not run again. Sam served the remainder of the war."

And he marched proudly with the other veterans.

Bill, who told me he was born in 1900, was a member of a family that was "into" history. The family had lived in Cheraw for generations, and a number of Bill's relatives had vivid memories of serving in the Civil War and of "surviving" the aftermath of the Reconstruction. Let me assure you, those people treasured the Southern Cause, and they neither forgave nor forgot.

Bill was a surveyor. In that business, as in many others, there are periods when business is so good you can't get it all done, and you can't leave. And then there are times when the reverse is true, when business is so bad you can't afford to leave.

Occasionally, however, the gods smiled and Bill had both time and money. When that happened, he loved to take off for a Civil War battlefield. He delighted in getting out on the terrain that had been fought over, map in hand, to try and visualize what the combatants saw.

Once in the early 1930s, Bill was at Gettysburg, that famous decisive battle that denied the Southern forces their last chance to wring victory from defeat. It was cold and raw February weather, and Bill was almost the only visitor at the site. He was there three days, tramping up and down, referring to his map and compass. There was one other observer there at the same time also sighting and studying and thinking. They never spoke, but at the end of the three days, each decided to return to his car at the same time, and they fell into step. Bill introduced himself, and the other man volunteered his name as Erwin Rommel of the German army.

Bill recalled that meeting in 1942 and 1943 when the papers were full of the successes (and failures) of the Desert Fox.

The Pee Dee River flows east across the northern counties of eastern and central South Carolina, moving sluggishly between low, swampy banks and sandbars, making it difficult to find a crossing where there is no bridge. For much of the history of the state, the bridge at Cheraw was the only one spanning the Pee Dee between the ocean and Salisbury, North Carolina.

In March 1865, retreating Confederates burned that bridge, causing the Union Army to spend three days in and around Cheraw. General Sherman and his chief officers chose the large houses in Cheraw for their use while here.

Sherman himself took over the ground floor of the house at 143 McIver (pronounced McKeever) Street for his personal headquarters. He took his meals there, allowing the McIver family to feed themselves after he and his officers had finished their meal.

There is a tale that Sherman was quite taken with little Eddie, a young son of the McIvers. The feeling was mutual, and the young boy often sat in the general's lap. One day Eddie was feeling around Sherman's head, and he exclaimed, "Mama! No horns!" The general loved it.

THE 1941 MANEUVERS

In another war, the bridge across the Pee Dee at Cheraw again proved its importance. The bridge was the strategic objective of the opposing US armies, who were testing tactics of infantry opposing tanks.

The "Blue" army held Cheraw that day but was forced to hurriedly retreat due to an encircling movement by the "Red" army, led by General George Patton. The Blue army command post had been in the old armory, but those officers took refuge in my family's back-yard. When Daddy arrived home from the store, he invited them into the house. They escaped under the cover of darkness. More excitement!

The troops in the Red and Blue armies were National Guard troops who were on tem-porary active duty for the maneuvers. When Pearl Harbor was attacked a few days later in December 1941, the "temporary" was deleted from their orders. They served four more years, for the duration of the conflict.

A communications unit arrived in our area a month before the maneuvers began and remained for a month after it was over. They bivouacked a couple of miles from Cheraw. That first day the company commander drove into town and called on the mayor. He promised the mayor that he would do all in his power to see that his men would be good citizens while here. In addition, he told the mayor that he had four young lieutenants in his company—young, single, well-behaved college graduates. Vouching for their good behavior, he asked for the mayor's help finding nice young women for them to date. The mayor agreed and secured blind dates for the four officers.

My cousin Helen and Walt were not together that first night, but after that they were a twosome. After Pearl Harbor, the unit was sent to the South Pacific for four years. Cousin Helen, accompanied by her mother, drove to New York. Walt got a three-day pass, and they were married. She came back and waited in Cheraw until he returned in late 1945. They were happily married for forty years.

In the latter weeks of 1944, my father was with a group of officers in New York waiting to be transferred to Europe. He could receive telephone calls but was not allowed to call out. Somehow, he got word to Mother that she should call him at a certain number. In those days, there was no area code or direct dialing. Every call had to go through at least one operator.

Mother's soft little low-country brogue was like a foreign language to the New York operator who was heavy on the Rs—"Parrrdon?"

Finally the connection was made, and the operator said, "Here's your parrrty, Madam, but if he can't understand you any better than I can, it won't do you any good!"

TALES OF "FESSOR" McCOWN

Professor J. K. McCown came to Cheraw in 1919 or 1920. He was a graduate of The Citadel and a veteran of the war in France.

It was customary in those days to refer to male teachers as "Professor." as a formality. After a very short time in Cheraw, Mr. McCown was awarded the affectionate term of "Fessor" by students , faculty, and the people on the street.

Interviewers on news programs today also use the term "professor". Mr. McCown was addressed by the *affectionate* term of "Fessor" by students, faculty, and the man on the street or in the pew.

He eventually became superintendent of the Cheraw School District and became responsible to the school board for all phases of education in the Cheraw public schools He hired and supervised the teachers and was in charge of the buildings, books, athletics, student discipline, and more. The year I left high school, 1948, was the first year the superintendent had any administrative help—even a secretary!

There are many stories about Fessor and most of them are affectionate. A lot of my tales come from Bernard Stubbs, who was one of his biggest tormentors—and one of his most devoted admirers. Bernard was at least as mischievous as the next guy and as willing as the next guy to steal a moment of pleasure; yet, in story after story he obeys Fessor's orders because "you don't mess with Fessor.".

On December 8, 1941, the day after the bombing of Pearl Harbor, Fessor had all the boys in the high school meet him on the infield of the baseball diamond adjacent to the school.

Fessor, being a realist, knew that most of them would be in service in a year or two and he began teaching them close order drill to prepare them for entry into the military (Nobody was going to get ahead of his boys!)

The budget was always tight for athletics. Team buses had not been thought of, nor would they have been affordable if they had been thought of. Usually the players went to out-of-town games with fans that were going to see the games. Fessor usually took his car, but the players tried to avoid riding with him because he was such a slow driver. He was a poor driver , so maybe it was a blessing that he drove slowly.

One day a mule got in the highway in front of Fessor's car. The boys swear they followed that mule down the highway all the way from Bennettsville to Clio, ten miles away!

Yet another time, Fessor had a car full of ballplayers returning from a game in Darlington. Turning on a road that led to his cousin's farm, Fessor pulled his car up to the house and told the boys he wanted to speak to his cousin and would return shortly. They waited and waited, then waited some more. Finally one of the boys got out of the car and crept up to the porch. Through the window he could see Fessor eating supper with his cousin. He had forgotten all about the boys in the car!

In the early 1940s Cheraw had a really good football team. One year they steamrolled the opposition for the first six or seven games. The team began to think quite a lot of themselves and that they could go through the season undefeated and maybe win the state championship. Then they went to Dillon with that cocky attitude and were trounced. They played poorly, with no pep or energy. They embarrassed themselves to such an extent that they agreed that none of them would show up for school the following Monday.

Bernard said he felt a hand on his shoulder as he lay in bed that next school day. He said, "Mama, I'm not going to school today."

A voice came back, "I'm not your mother, Stubbs. Now get dressed and I'll see you at school." Bernard hurriedly got up and dressed, and when he got to school, he found the other members of the team already there. Fessor had visited them all!

That same group, who must have possessed a gargantuan imagination, organized the Cheraw Chapter of the National Hooky Society. The National Honor Society, also known as NHS, was composed of the outstanding juniors and seniors at the school and was unswerving in following rules. The National Hooky Society was different.

The National Hooky Society met on an irregular basis once or twice a month, at a location disclosed at the last minute. One time, in spite of their precautions, Fessor got wind of their plans. After the boys had gathered at the river, Fessor arrived in his car and told them to report back to school. They all did, because nobody messes with Fessor!

Another time, the same group came together because they didn't want to go to school on Easter Monday. They decided to stage a sit-down strike to dramatize their demand for a holiday. On the appointed day they remained out in the schoolyard after recess and did not return to class. It was not long before Fessor appeared to find out what was happening. One of the leaders explained their desire for an Easter Monday holiday and their determination not to attend classes until their demand was met. Fessor pulled out his pocket watch and announced, "Anyone not in class at twelve forty-five can have all the holidays he wants, beginning tomorrow." The strikers disintegrated.

Believe it or not, there is another story involving this same crowd of mischief-makers. One Sunday afternoon someone noticed that a cow belonging to a neighbor of the school was staked out on the athletic field eating the grass. Someone else thought it would be fun to put the cow in the schoolhouse. With two boys guiding each leg, plus one boy leading and one pushing from the rear, they led her into the school and up the stairs into the second floor hallway. There they left her, feeling sure the cow's mess would bring them a holiday on Monday while the place was cleaned up.

The next morning they reported to school, sure they would not be there long. Fessor called all the boys together and said, "I'm not sure how you boys got this cow up here. I'm going to go to my office and shut the door for thirty minutes. If the cow is not out of this school in that length of time, there will be an investigation and several will be expelled." With that, Fessor turned and went into his office.

The boys led her down the steps and outside using the same methods they had employed to get her in the school in the first place. There was no investigation, and no one was punished.

I told this story to a group of adults. They all chuckled. Afterward, a retired minister who had grown up in Cheraw approached me. I had heard, from his contemporaries, that he had been a "handful" as a teenager. He asked me, "Hal, do you think this really happened?" I replied that I thought so but had no names. He replied, with a twinkle, "It didn't happen in my time, or I would have been in on it."

The custodian at the school during most of those years was a faithful colored man named John Ellerbe. He was attentive and loyal to Fessor, but at the same time he could see the humor in the tricks those boys played on the man.

One day Fessor was preparing to go to the Kiwanis meeting for lunch, so he parked his car outside the side door of the school. A couple of boys spotted it, found some empty Coke crates, and placed the crates under the rear bumper so that the wheels would not reach the ground. Fessor came out, got in his car, cranked it, and put it in gear. The engine roared, but the car did not move. Fessor tried again, with no result. Finally, he went inside to get help from John Ellerbe. John spotted the crates and removed them, and Fessor drove off this meeting. As soon as he was out of sight, John convulsed with laughter.

Fessor found several boys who had cut typing class downtown at the pool hall. He directed them to meet him in his office at the school. They all reported in because nobody messes with Fessor. He began to pace up and down as he talked to them, trying to impress on each of them the value of an education. To one of the boys he said, "Why, Otis, all your grades together don't add up to one hundred!" The boy replied, "No, Fessor, that's not right! You're talking about the *other* Otis!"

Fessor was a devoted Kiwanis member. For many years he was secretary-treasurer. Once he was installing Bob as a new member and told him that the average member paid his dues by the year and in advance. Bob reached in his pocket and pulled out the dues for the year. Fessor accepted the money and said, "Congratulations, Bob. You're the very first man to come up to the average!"

Prior to the 1950s the state provided very little in the way of books and teaching aids for the black schools. Fessor understood that they were deprived because he and the local black

educators met regularly to discuss mutual problems. Fessor gave or loaned books and other
materials to the black schools from any excess
or surplus he could find. This was greatly appre-
ciated by the black teachers, and they invited
Fessor to speak to their upper classes on the
subject of "Leadership". Introducing him, the
black principal told of Fessor's credentials and
his history of being helpful to the black schools.
"His face may be white," he said, "but his heart
is just as black as yours!"

Small towns breed indelible characters,
and lots of them, almost as fast as mosquitoes

multiply after frequent showers. Tales accumulate around the special ones, like the stories I'm going to relate now. There are many more stories, but these are among the most interesting, and, to the best of my knowledge, they are all true.

STRAWS IN
THE WIND

In the early days we lived on Third Street in a big house that had a large magnolia tree on the corner of the lot. That magnolia, with its limbs closely spaced, was perfect for kids five- to ten-years-old to climb. It was often a magnet that drew the neighborhood to gather there.

One morning the magnolia was full of kids, and my mother was sitting on the front porch working on something while she watched us. Suddenly a new sound punctuated the air, and she realized that somebody was falling out of the tree. She could hear the body bouncing off limbs as it descended. She reached the foot of the tree just about the same time Billy did. He bounced off the lowest limb and landed on his back. He looked up at her, grinned, and said, "I didn't miss a one, did I?" He was unhurt but walked home to count his bruises. He was back in the tree after lunch.

Back then we had the freedom of the neighborhood. Little ones were forbidden to cross the street, but big kids could ride bikes anywhere (in the neighborhood) without special permission. In those un-air-conditioned days, windows and doors were open. Since few mothers worked outside the home, *somebody's* mother was sure to be looking out the window at any given time. Most neighborhood mothers felt they had spanking privileges with the neighborhood children (and they were willing to assert themselves if they felt it necessary). And most mothers shared the same thinking: "Of course, the Lindbergh child was kidnapped, but they didn't live in Cheraw," so worries about kidnapped children were not widespread. What I call "The Mothers' Brigade" worked well.

Here's an example of the Mothers' Brigade. When Amaryllis was in the fifth grade, she often rode her bike to school. One day her teacher asked her to ride her "wheel" to the teacher's house, pick up a package the maid would give her, and bring it to school.

She gladly ran the errand and returned to school twenty minutes later to find her mother there waiting for her. Miss Julia had received three phone calls from mothers who had seen Amaryllis riding her bike during school hours!

The Mothers' Brigade should have been looking out the window when a group of boys marched off to the woods at Sliding Hill to engage in a war with BB guns (air rifles). Several were hit in the eye.

Al is not my oldest friend (many of my friends are old.) but this fellow has been my friend since before I entered first grade. That's a pretty good stretch of time. There came a time in his life when he needed to downsize; his wife was gone, his children were gone, and his big house was full of furniture. He gave his children what furniture they would take. He sold some pieces, set aside the furniture he would take with him when he moved to smaller quarters, and resolved to give the remainder away.

When give-away day came, he hauled the first load to the curb and went back to the house to get the next. While inside, he glanced out the window and saw a neighbor pull over to examine the furniture. He continued gathering together the next load, and when he next looked out the window, his initial load had disappeared. Pleased, he hauled his next batch of furniture to the curb. This time, he hardly got back in the house before the neighbor was loading his "treasure" to its new home. The third load was handled differently: Al loaded it into his own car, drove to his neighbor's house, put his load of unwanted furniture on the front porch, and rang the bell. When the door opened, my friend put his hand on his hip and said, "Thought I'd save you a trip."

Years ago when we were single and foolish (imagine!) he and I were invited to a house party at True Blue Creek House on Pawley's Island. We spent a lazy afternoon sitting on a wide screen porch gazing across the salt marsh that separates the mainland from the island. We discussed (and solved) the affairs of the world, drinking beer and throwing the empty cans into a wheelbarrow conveniently placed on the porch by our host. After two or three hours of this, my friend stood up and excused himself, saying, "I've got beer between all my teeth!"

In a historic occasion, a young Cheraw woman named Pattie volunteered to sit in the front window of The Women's Shop while she received Cheraw's first permanent wave. Passersby lined the sidewalk, watching while she sat under a peculiar-looking contraption like a floor lamp, with the "shade" coming down over her head.

When I was in college I was on the swim team. In one meet, we were fortunate enough to defeat the team from the University of South Carolina. The newspaper gave a good bit of space to cover this unusual event, and there was a big photo of me with the article. Of course I sent a copy of the article home to my folks, and *of course* Mother carried the paper around in her purse for *weeks*.

One day she wanted to show it to a female relative, but the lady would not look until she had used her hands to obscure the skin that was prominent above and below my skimpy racing suit. "First, let's cover up his nakedness," she said.

Cheraw's most famous citizen is surely John Birks Gillespie, known all over the world as "Dizzy," the inventor of bebop. He was born in Cheraw around 1917, and lived with his parents on Huger Street. An irrepressible cutup, he told somebody his father beat him with a leather strap every day, "because he said he knew I'd done something to deserve it." In spite of that parental attitude, John Birks developed into a happy, cheerful fellow. He had music in his veins, and by the age of eight was playing trumpet at parties and dances for white people—in the segregated South.

As a teenager he won a music scholarship to the Laurinburg Institute, thirty miles away. After completing his studies there, he found his way to Philadelphia. His trumpet was bent during an accident, and soon Dizzy and his bent trumpet became internationally famous. Each time he played, he introduced himself as "John Birks Gillespie, from Cheraw, South Carolina."

Bessie was an eighty-two-year-old black woman who still worked one day a week for one of Am's mother's friends. She had worked for Am's mother when Am was a preschooler. One day, while on a visit to Georgetown, Am encountered Bessie. "Amaryllis, you bes more like yo' daddy eb'ry time I see you. In fac', the older you gets, the wusser you look like him!"

Miss Julia, Am's mother, was constantly on the lookout for "used furniture" she could transform into "antiques" with a little repair and polish. She made regular forays into the countryside and found that colored families would often be willing to sell a piece for cash. Miss Julia was accompanied on these shopping trips by a colored lady who served as liaison. The lady suffered a stroke and disappeared from circulation for a time. Then one day Miss

Julia saw her on the sidewalk and asked how she was getting along.

"Pretty good, Miss Julia," she said, "but sometimes I stagnate like a 'toxicant man'!"

There was a stubby little black man around town who had a physical condition that caused him to bend over from the waist unless he could hold on to something for support. He was an industrious fellow and a frequent visitor at our store. When he needed credit, he would present himself to me and ask, "Mr. Duvall, is my face clean?" Which was to say, "Is my credit good today?"

Sister grew up on a farm in the neighboring county. After their marriage, she and her husband became citizens of Cheraw. One day her father took her for a ride in his car. Returning to the farm, she was horrified and frightened when he turned left across the busy highway to enter his driveway.

"Daddy! She remonstrated, "This is the busiest north-south highway in Marlboro County! You've got to give a signal when you turn left like that!"

"Hell, Sister," he replied. "Everybody knows where I live."

George had been a tractor driver and over-seer all his life, working for two different farm-ers who both retired before George, then sev-enty, was ready to quit. He then found a job he liked with the Street Department of the Town of Cheraw. The two of us had been on friendly terms for years and continued to speak pleas-antly to each other when our paths crossed.

One day I was returning from a trip to the post office and walked through a green area that George and his crew were raking. "Hold on there, fellow," said George, with a mock stern face and a grin. "Don't walk through here where we're working!" "But, George, I'm just trying to get back to the store the quickest way."

"Well, OK then, but move along. I don't want to have to run you in."

Two girls were born to a family in the Pee Dee region. They were the most identical twins anyone had ever seen. Their parents liked the sensation these girls caused, so each day they saw that they were dressed in identical outfits.

When the girls married, one twin lived in Marion and the other lived in Conway. True to their training, each morning they conversed on the phone and coordinated their outfits for the day. Still, with the possible exception of their husbands, no one could tell the twins apart.

One morning in the grocery store, a friend greeted one of the twins. "Hello! Is that you, or is it your sister?"

"It's my sister."

My father was not a funny man like his brother Hiney. He enjoyed a good joke but did not tell them. He was a wonderful teacher and a goal-oriented man, whether in school or in business.

Back in the 1960s, Daddy got a bad medical report and was told to report to Medical

University Hospital for treatment. In those days, medical insurance was not common. Daddy had no insurance. The hospital was very specific and insistent that he bring a certain amount of cash to deposit when he was admitted.

The surgery was performed successfully, and after recuperation he was told he could go home. "Where's my bill?" he asked.

"Oh, don't worry about it, Mr. Duvall. They're working on your statement, and we'll send you a bill in a few days."

"I would like to have my bill."

"That's all right, sir. You go on home and we'll send it to you."

Daddy got dressed and went to the office. Again he asked for his bill. His request was deflected again.

Without another word, Daddy walked across the room and took a seat in one of the chairs that were lined against the wall.

Thirty minutes later, one of the workers looked up and noticed him sitting there. "Why, Mr. Duvall, you're still here," she said, surprised. "You can go on home now."

Daddy said, "When I came in, you wouldn't admit me without my cash being deposited with you. I'm not going to leave until I get my bill."

He had to wait a little while as they scurried around, but he got the bill.

There is a registered nurse who worked for years in the operating room in one of the local hospitals. She's a capable nurse who knows her profession. I imagine she's a pleasure to work with, because she's more than a little irreverent.

They tell me the surgeon did a circumcision on a patient. Everything went well and the repaired man was returned to his room where his wife and mother waited. The patient eventually "woke up" enough to remember what had happened. He raised the sheet off his chest, took a look, and emitted a loud groan! The women rushed to his side to help any way they could. He pointed under the sheet. They looked and discovered he had been decorated with a red bow ribbon! The surgeon declared he was not involved.

Proclaimed as "The World's Largest Cocktail Party," the Carolina Cup is a steeplechase, a horse race where the horses are required to jump over obstacles as well as run fast. It is held in Camden each spring, usually around Easter. There was a group from Cheraw that attended one year in the mid-1950s.

There were several married couples in the group, veterans of the physical demands made by an entire day of eating, drinking, and having fun. In addition to the couples, the group also included a couple of neophyte single men who lacked the experience and stamina to handle the pressure of so much pleasure. The group parked in the infield, opened the trunk, opened the bar, opened the picnic baskets brought by the women, and commenced.

There were horses there and horse races (steeplechases, excuse me!), but that group paid little attention to them. They greeted acquaintances who strolled by, laughed and talked, and poured another drink.

By early afternoon every member of the group had located the Porta-Potties that had been stationed around the infield. On one of his trips, one member of the group noticed a very attractive woman sitting alone in the back seat of a car. He was normally a shy individual, but under the influence of food and drink he approached the car to get a closer look. She looked up and smiled. He smiled back. They had a nice conversation for a few minutes, and he asked for her name and phone number. He pulled a piece of paper out of his wallet and wrote what she dictated. He bade her adieu and continued to the Porta-Potty.

This guy laughingly told me that while cleaning out his wallet he found a scrap of paper with something like Egyptian hieroglyphics written on it. "Couldn't make out a thing!" he said. Then it occurred to him that this must be the name, address, and phone number of the beautiful girl at the Carolina Cup!

A number of banks did business in Cheraw in the 1920s, and I think every one of them failed in that dreadful decade. This caused a tremendous lifestyle change for everybody in town, including the owners of the banks. The wife of the owner of one of the failed .banks told her longtime colored housekeeper she would have to let her go. The housekeeper replied that she had some money saved and would be glad to let her employer have it, if she could stay on and help.

There was a black man we used to see walking on Greene Street—though I should say "marching," not "walking." He was a veteran of either World War I or the Spanish-American War (I've heard it both ways). He used to march, erect, walking briskly as if on parade.

We young boys used to sneak up behind him and march along, too. He would suddenly whirl around, "to the rear, March!" If he found us behind him (and he knew we were there) he would brandish his stick and we would run like the devil.

Back in the early days when Frank Howard was newly installed as head football coach at Clemson College, the atmosphere on the sidelines was more like a family than a business. Fathers of players were even allowed to sit on the bench with the team.

There was a father from Pawley's Island, famous for his reputation as a fisherman as well as for his colorful profanity, whose son was a third-string quarterback on the team. One day at Memorial Stadium, Clemson had cruised to a three-touchdown lead against a North Carolina team, and Coach Howard decided to insert that third-string quarterback in the game. His father, sitting on the team bench, sat up straight and preened himself with pride.

On the first play, the third-stringer stumbled over his own feet and fell ignominiously to the ground, losing three yards. His father was on his feet in an instant, tugging urgently at the sleeve of Frank Howard. "Take the sumbitch out, Coach! Take him out!"

There was a rich widow in our town. (At least *we* thought she was rich. She may have disagreed.) Her husband had been dead for a good many years, and she ran her large farm with a firm hand. In fact, she ran *everything* with a firm hand, stating her opinions and brooking no argument. Her neighbors knew, from experience, that she was a kind person, but everyone else was afraid of her gruff ways.

The widow had a little dog what went everywhere with her. "Little Bit" was adored. In the car, she rode in the widow's lap looking out the window as they drove along. When her Chevrolet was approaching its "last legs," the widow attempted to trade it in for a similar car, but Little Bit couldn't see out of the window of the newer model. The resourceful dealer sold her a Cadillac so Little Bit could see out the window!

When the dog died, the widow was inconsolable. She purchased a child's casket, and Little Bit was laid to rest in the widow's family plot in St. David's Cemetery. Many townspeople were incensed over this. There was so much anger and controversy that a kind neighbor offered to go to the cemetery at night, dig up the casket, and re-bury it in his yard, next door to the widow. She accepted his offer, and it was done!

My grandmother Farmer, Mother's mother, was treasurer of a tiny Episcopal Church in tiny Allendale, South Carolina, in the early days of the twentieth century. Her husband, my thgrandfather, was resident of the only bank in town.

The little church's treasury amounted to a grand total of thirty-nine dollars. The rules of the church directed her to deposit the church funds in a bank. She, as the wife of the bank president, knew how precarious the bank's finances were, so she faced a dilemma. Should she play by the rules, deposit the money in the bank, and possibly lose it if the bank goes under, or should she keep the money at home?

She thought about it, worried about it, prayed about it. In the end, she decided to keep her mouth shut and keep the church's money in her purse, where it would be safe.

Melvin is a gentle, slow-moving, quiet black man who does "odd jobs" for many households around Cheraw. He will tackle almost anything. Because of his willing nature, he is assigned a variety of tasks, from gardening to painting to cleaning to moving furniture. Like most of us, though, Melvin is not perfect. If his budget gets a dollar or two ahead, he is more likely to spend it on liquor than food. That, as Satchel Paige once said, "angries up the stomach."

The money should have been given to his divorced wife for her support, as ordered by the court. If he had done this instead, he would have avoided being brought into court and sentenced to serve in the county jail for nonsupport.

One of his clients, and a loyal supporter, was a white lady called "Miss Martha." They were neighbors, living a stone's throw from each other (if you were Satchel Paige at least). She tried her best to look after him, making sure he had enough food and advice.

One day he told her he had been summoned to appear before the judge for nonpayment of support, so she volunteered to give him a ride to the courthouse. Upon arriving, she took a seat in the back, and Melvin sat in the place that was reserved for offenders. When his case was called, he was found guilty of nonsupport and sentenced to sixty days in the county jail.

There was a wail from the back. "Nooooo!" Miss Martha marched up the aisle and spoke indignantly to her neighbor, the judge. "How do you expect him to earn any money for support if he's in jail for sixty days?" Turning to the black man, she said, "Come on, Melvin, we're going home!" And Melvin followed her out the door and into her car. Two hours later, a deputy drove up to Melvin's house and took him to the county jail.

The next day, Miss Martha phoned Melvin's clients and raised money to pay his fine. Each paid her share, including the wife of the judge.

When Miss Martha arrived at the county jail to pay Melvin's fine, she was recognized by a number of other inmates, and was greeted be a chorus of "Hello, Miss Martha."

Some time later, Melvin suffered a ssevere stroke and was admitted to Veterans' Hospital. After a period of time, Miss Martha sent her son-in-law to check on him. When the son-in-law entered the ward, he saw a sign that limited visiting privileges to family members only. He had brought Melvin some ice cream, so he pulled up a chair beside the bed and began feeding Melvin the ice cream, one spoon at a time. An attendant came up and asked the white visitor if he was a family member. "Yes," said the visitor and never missed a beat with the spoon.

Frank was a colored gentleman about my parents' age. He had gone to work for a family on Market Street as a yard boy when he was twelve, and he stayed there until he died. He developed into a good gardener. Every day he milked their cow, invariably called "Sugar Babe." He drove their car and ran errands. He cooked. At the big meal of the day, two o'clock in the afternoon, he donned a starched white mess jacket and served the table. He served breakfast in bed to those who wanted it.

Later, a grandson of the lady of the house came to stay there because his father was overseas with the Navy. The kid had never been around many men. He adored Frank and used to follow him around the house and yard. One day the young boy said, "Frank, are you my granddaddy?" "No, Tim," Frank replied, "but I love you like I was."

Here follows my all-time favorite true story. I've told it before, in print, in the opening chapter of *Juniper Road*. If you read it there and don't care to do it again, just skip it and go on to the next. But, I think it's a story worth retelling—and rereading.

Wilson's father was in the hospital with tuberculosis. He and his mother lived *gratis* in a relative's tenant house, with no money and little food. It was the dark days of the

Depression. The fourteen-year-old boy heard of a government program hiring axmen for a dollar a day, so he shouldered his ax and walked to the advertised hiring place. There he found a long line of men, snaking its way toward a man sitting at a table in the shade of a tree. The boy took his place at the end of the line, and finally he was at the front. The interviewer looked up, took in the young face and slender frame at a glance, and kindly asked, "How old are you, son?" The boy bravely lied, "I'll be sixteen in two weeks." Taking pity on the boy, who obviously needed the job, he asked, "Do you think you can be eighteen by Monday?" "Yes, sir!" was the quick reply. "Then come back Monday."

A former resident of Cheraw, now eighty-five years old, returned to Cheraw from Miami for a family funeral. Chatting with the funeral director at the funeral home, the visitor said, "You know, I'm one of your prime prospects." To a couple who were standing nearby and overheard, he added, "I've always thought it would be nice to die in the springtime, because there are so many flowers." The unknown lady replied, "Well, my flowers are beginning to fade now. Wait until next year."

Ol' Albert was custodian at the local bank for many years and was on good conversational terms with its customers. One day he was asked, "How's your wife?" "Lawd, Boss," he replied. "When I married that woman I coulda eat' her up! Now I wish to God I had."

One of my favorite customers in our store was an industrious black man named Tom. Tom enjoyed reminiscing and I was an eager audience. He told me that one of his first jobs was shining shoes on the streets of Cheraw when he was a kid. "I had all the different colors of polish, could handle those light-colored two-tone shoes Dr. Purvis wore, and didn't get no polish on his socks, neither." And, "a good 'pop rag' can change a ten-cent shine into a quarter shine with one or two 'pops.'"

"Another job I had was starting fires in white folks' houses before going to school. I'd start a fire in every fireplace before they got up, then come back by after school to fill up the wood box and do anything else they wanted. Sometime they'd feed me, too."

Tom eventually settled into the coal and wood business when he grew up. One winter day I asked him if he'd had a good Christmas. "Oh, yessuh, I did. Bill came by the house Christmas morning needin' some money, so the two of us cut wood all that day. Yessuh. Had a good Christmas."

When blacks received the right to vote, Tom became a "hauler" rounding up people in his neighborhood and taking them to the polls—and, incidentally, instructing them for whom to vote.

He had a vegetable garden and a little store. I always intended to visit his store with a tape recorder to preserve some his history, but he died before I got around to it. That's too bad, because Tom's stories were interesting.

Johnny, one of our regular customers, was happily telling me one day about his new Labrador puppy. He was training the pup to be a retriever and was very excited with his progress. One day he decided to take the puppy with him when he went fishing. Johnny got the dog and all his other paraphernalia in the boat and pushed out from shore. Johnny brought out his rod, fit a lure to the line, and cast out into the lake. No sooner had he cast the lure than the puppy sprang from the boat, swam to the lure, and swam back to his master with the lure in his mouth. Unfortunately, the dog did not know how to get back in the boat, so Johnny had to get into the water, boost the puppy back into the boat, and then get himself back in. He gave the dog stern instructions *not* to retrieve a fishing lure; then, holding the dog with one arm, he cast again. The animal burst from his arms and into the water he went, determined to get that lure. Johnny gave up and returned home. "Boss, when this one gives out I've got another one in the garage, a new one, all paid for, that I'm going to use."

Willie was the iceman, delivering blocks of ice to houses that used iceboxes instead of the new electric refrigerators. He had a gimpy leg, greatly bowed from some accident that did not tolerate self-healing. He drove an ancient pickup truck and worked his route through the streets of Cheraw. When I was about six or seven, I was riding my bike on the sidewalk of Kershaw Street when my attention was caught by the sight of a big black billy goat emerging from the backyard of a house across the street. He was trailing the rope and the stake that were intended to keep him in the yard. I was fascinated by the sight of this evil-looking creature and stopped my bike to watch him. He apparently thought the little white boy was interesting, too, for he continued to approach me. When he reached me and my bike, he proceeded to walk around us, still trailing the rope. Soon I was effectively hog-tied, and as soon as I realized it, I began to cry.

Fortunately for me, "the iceman cometh." Willie jumped out of his pickup truck, limped over to us, unwound the goat's rope from the helpless captives, and returned the goat to its owner. I thanked him, and whenever we saw each other from then on we called each other "Goat."

This next tale is about a man I did not know personally, though my dad knew him. We bought fence, nails, and roofing every week for our store from his supply company.

One Sunday in the mid-1950s, Cheraw was visited by a savage little hailstorm that inflicted damage to many roofs in the community. Two or three days later, Daddy received a letter from our supplier. "Dear Hal, As you may know, I have a sister who lives in Cheraw. She contacted me this week with the news that her roof had been damaged by a hailstorm. Yesterday our truck delivered shingles to her house so the roof can be repaired. Enclosed is a credit memorandum to compensate you for the profit you would have realized if I had not given the shingles to her."

What a gentleman!

In the glorious post-war days, a wonderful new industry decided to locate a plant in

Cheraw. We were ecstatic over the prospect of salaries and jobs for our little town. The first plant manager was a real smoothie and soon had all the townspeople eating out of his hand. After a few years, this manager was transferred somewhere else and a new man took his place. He was apparently capable, very straightforward, plainspoken, and on top of things—but to the outsider who didn't work for him, he appeared to lack the smiling charm of his predecessor. One day I was chatting with one of the plant's middle management people, and I asked him how he liked the new plant manager. Before answering, he looked around to see who might be listening. Then he said, "If the first guy called you into his office and talked to you for fifteen minutes, when you left you weren't sure whether you'd been chewed out or patted on the back." He continued, "Now, you know."

One of my old customers, now ninety, was talking to me about his two sisters, aged eighty-five and ninety-five. "They both still drive their own cars," he said. "I just bought a new car for my ninety-five-year-old sister; in fact, I've bought her last five cars for her. I'll tell you, she was mighty good to me when I needed help and I've tried not to forget it. It was 1930. I had just finished Wofford College and couldn't get a job anywhere. I worked at a gas station in Charlotte for twelve hours a day, seven days a week, for sixty dollars a month. Then I was night watchman at a tobacco warehouse in Mullins for seventy-five dollars a month. Then my older sister, who was a school teacher in Hartsville, heard about a highway paving project from the North Carolina line to Bennettsville. She, a real go-getter, sold me to the road contractor, sight unseen! My widowed mother lived in Clio so I could live with her. The only trouble was, I had no transportation, no way to get to work. This same sister had an old Ford, so she traded it in for a new one. She turned the new car over to me to go to work in, and she walked to school! I tell you, I've tried not to forget that!"

We had an interesting principal at the "grammar school"(first through seventh grades) just before World War II. He was in charge of discipline, plus he taught several classes. One day in class he asked a question of a student who replied, "I don't know, Mr. Baker." "Humph," said the principal. "Honest confession is good for the soul. I'll give you one hundred!"

Bo grew up following the north end of a southbound mule in the Cash community. His boss, recognizing Bo's gentle dependability, promoted him to be yardman at the boss's home in Cheraw. From there he changed jobs twice, and when I knew him, he was driving his old pickup for a local industry, running errands, getting the mail, making small retail purchases downtown, and doing anything else he was asked to do. He drove his own elderly pickup, but he told me, "Boss, when this one gives out I've got another one in the garage, a new one, all paid for, that I'm going to use."

Bo was invariably pleasant. When he entered our store, he bade "good morning" to each person who worked there. He was particularly careful to speak to Miss Carolyn, who ran the office, taking off his cap when he said "Good morning, Miss."

Bo couldn't read, but he had an excel-lent memory. He was given notes for the salespeople who would be serving him. Bo couldn't count, either, but he could save money. About twice a year he appeared at the back door of Miss Carolyn's house dressed in his Sunday best—a blue pin-stripe suit. Snatching off his hat, he would say, "Miss, would you do something for me? Would you count my money for me?" And he handed her a paper bag filled with bills. He waited outside while she went inside, counted the money, and reported the total. "Thank you, Miss. I thought that was about right. Do I owe you anything?" He trusted her not to cheat him. In my opinion, he knew how much money was supposed to be there, and he was checking to make sure no one had found his stash.

Bo gave out before his old pickup did. I miss him.

My wife Jean's grandmother, "Gramps", twice widowed, managed to raise five children in the poorest part of Georgia. It was called the "kerosene belt" because electricity came to those farmers long after everyone else had been served. When Jean's mother was also widowed, "Gramps" came to live with them, taking over the housekeeping so Jean's mother could take a full-time job. Gramps loved the soap operas on TV and managed to watch them most days. One New Year's Day, when Jean and I and the children were at their house, Gramps turned on the television to watch her program but a football game was on. She tried again after lunch but again found a football game. When she tried to watch the evening news and then Lawrence Welk but still finding football, she declared, "I know those boys are worn out! They have been running and jumping all day long!"

My high school classmate had a wonder-ful career as an engineer with General Electric, working all over the world. He retired and returned to Cheraw in time to attend our fif-tieth class reunion. As part of the evening's program, we were each asked to   tell the class about our family and career. The engineer was the last to be called on. "If you people," he said, "think I'm going to tell you what I've been doing for the last fifty years, you're crazy as hell!" And he sat down.

Five years later, at the fifty-fifth reunion, the same procedure was followed. This time, the engineer reported, "Well, I brought you up to date five years ago." That brought down the house.

My mother had several close friends. One particular friendship spanned fifty years. They walked together, played cards together, shared family secrets and problems (some, anyway), and shared gossip. One of their shared interests was girdles. You know—those tight, elastic, figure-shaping undergarments some women wore to keep their stockings up. My mother often exclaimed, "Oh, I love my girdle! It helps my back!" I doubt, though, if anyone has ever heard of a woman who loved her *new* girdle. They tell me the term "uncomfortable" is not a strong enough word.

Mother's friend confided that she had gotten a new girdle a month ago and had worn it only twice. "My old one is my friend. It's comfortable, but this new thing is an instrument of the devil." The subject came up again a month later. Mother's friend confided that she still avoided wearing the new girdle but she had hit upon a plan that satisfied one of her worries.

"What are you worrying about?" Mother asked.

"I'm afraid I'll die during the night. If people come in to straighten up, they'll see that ratty-looking old girdle with the clothes I took off when I went to bed, and they'll say, 'Poor little Mrs. Jones! She didn't have enough money to wear decent underclothes! Poor woman!'"

And then a sly smile touched her lips. " I still have this new girdle in the drawer right here. At night when I undress, I put my old friendly girdle in this wastebasket and put the new girdle with my clothes in the chair! Then in the morning I get the old girdle out of the wastebasket and put the new one back in its box in the drawer."

"Miss Mat" was everybody's favorite first-grade teacher. In fact, from before 1900 and up to 1930, she was the only one in town. A maiden lady, she was a dedicated and well-loved teacher—though a bit old by the time she finished teaching. In the words of one of her later pupils, "She was past her prime when she got to us." She was so deaf she used an ear trumpet. Some of her pupils took advantage of that, moving their lips and pretending to read. She never heard a word, and never caught on.

Back in the days of the Great Depression, one of the new phrases we learned and used frequently was "New Deal." This was the collective term that was symbolic of the Democratic administration's multi-pronged efforts to find work for the unemployed. The Work Projects Administration, commonly called WPA, employed *anybody*, able-bodied, infirm, lazy, feeble, illiterate, it didn't seem to matter—and using these unskilled people, the WPA accomplished an amazing number of tasks building up the infrastructure across the country.

The WPA was the butt of a lot of jokes from scoffers, who only saw the work crews when they were on break and said WPA stood for "We Poke Along."

Then there's this probably untrue story about the local WPA crew chief who wired Washington, "We're out of shovel handles. Send us some handles." Washington wired back: "We're out of handles also. Lean on each other."

Early in the twentieth century, a family moved to Cheraw from Wisconsin and opened a lumber mill. The son married a local girl and remained here the rest of his life. He was active in community affairs, taking part in every worthwhile endeavor that came along. To many of us, he was "Mr. Cheraw."

He loved sports of all kinds and was asked to be master of seremonies at many sports celebrations held locally. At one sports banquet, he asked four young men to sing a few songs as a quartet, hoping to vary the evening and charm the crowd. When the singers finished and sat down, the MC rose from his chair and resumed the podium. He said, "Well, not as good as I'd hoped, but not as bad as I feared."

When Billy and I first encountered Action Comic Books and Superman, we were enthralled. We were nine or ten at the time and we couldn't wait for the next issue to come out. Of course, we didn't buy the book. We read it at Wannamaker's and put it back in the rack for somebody else to buy. The caption on the front cover of the books said, "Superman, a twentieth century creation." To a ten-year-old, the twentieth century obviously would begin in the year 2000. Doing some rapid mental arithmetic, we agreed that we would be seventy in the year 2000. When that day in the far distant future arrived, we agreed we would jump out of a second-story window and holler "Superman! Save me!" And of course he would come.

I called Billy in that target year and invited him to jump with me. He declined to participate, even with bungee cords. In his defense, you have to realize he's been sick.

Frank was a Middle-Easterner who worked his way to the United States on a freighter. He learned the restaurant trade in New Jersey and ended up in Cheraw running his own café. Frank's café experienced the same hard times everyone faced during the Depression. It was a one-man show; he had no other help, and he was having a difficult time keeping the place open.

Imagine his pleasure when he saw a big Buick pull up to the front of the café. Inside were four Yankee tourists headed for Florida and looking for breakfast. Frank ushered them, took their orders, and repeated them in a loud voice to the (imaginary) cook in the kitchen. He dashed back and forth between the dining room and the kitchen, trying to get it all together in an impressive manner. This resulted in so much delay that the tourists got up from the table and re-entered their car, prepared to drive away.

When Frank saw what was happening, he realized he was not going to be paid for the four breakfasts he had cooked. He was beside himself! He grabbed a butcher knife and attacked the tires of the car as it pulled away from the curb.

In court, Frank demanded "justice." His lawyer advised him to plead for "mercy."

Another time, Frank ordered six geese from a poultry broker to serve to his customers at Thanksgiving. He wanted them shipped by Railway Express, which was then the fastest shipping company in the country. A week before the holiday, he telephoned the local Railway Express agent. "Lewis," Frank said to his friend, not identifying himself, "you got dem goose?"

"What did you say?" asked Lewis, unaware of the problem—or that it was Frank talking to him.

"You get dem goose?" Frank repeated.

"You g— d— goose, yourself!" said the exasperated Lewis, slamming down the phone.

Another time, a friend discovered Frank taking a bath in the dishwashing sink.

In the 1890s, the bridge across the Pee Dee was washed away by a fierce flood. Without the bridge, a ferry was soon set up to assist people getting across. It was a "for profit" ferry.

One Saturday afternoon, the ferryman heard a shout from the Marlboro side. "Mr. Walter! Mr. Walter, come and get me! I wants to come to Cheraw."

"You got any money?" Mr. Walter wanted to know.

"Yessuh, I got a quarter."

"If you ain't got but a quarter, you might as well stay where you are."

I mentioned the Pegues fish traps in an earlier story. There are fish traps— basket-like contraptions that rotate vertically around an axle, powered by the current of the water. The first traps were placed in the Pee Dee by Native Americans to capture the shad, which came up the river to spawn each spring. The traps partially block the fishes' path and channel them into the reach of the revolving fish baskets, which pick up fish and throw them into retaining baskets. They have been rebuilt over the years, and I don't know if anyone is maintaining them now.

In my childhood days there was never any question about what we would do on Saturday afternoons. Western movies! Cowboy movies! The cowboys rode the range every Saturday. There was no trouble identifying the hero: He wore a white hat and generally had pearl-handled pistols. Stagecoaches, Indians, heroines in long dresses buttoned to the neck, and beautiful horses were always present in the best Cowboy stories. And you could always count on the hero having a bumbling sidekick who meant well. An added attraction was the serial, a story that left the hero at death's door each week so that we had to return for the next installment the following week to find out what happened. We could enter the theatre at 2:00 p.m. and stay until dark, seeing as many repetitions as we liked. There was a 9:oo p.m. horror show, but we didn't want to see that.Still don't.

And it was cheap! Admission to the theatre was eleven cents. Popcorn was a nickel. If you were lucky enough to begin the afternoon with a whole quarter, you could also go to "The Hole in the Wall"—a candy store where Mr. and Mrs. Gardner sold sweet delights for a penny, or two for a penny. An astute shopper could go home with pockets bulging, but obesity was not a problem for the active children we were.

The Lone Ranger had a radio show, and the William Tell Overture introduced each broadcast. Billy and I sent in our Merita bread labels along with a quarter and received our own secret ring and code. We had so much fun playing with those for weeks!

I didn't know Tom, but I heard the following story about him. Tom came from a family that lived in and around Cheraw a generation ahead of my time. Hearing that his brother was under the weather, he walked the few blocks to his brother's house to check on his condition. He found the sick man in bed with the sheet pulled up to his chin.

He deflected Tom's inquiry with a short reply, "Touch of the flu."

"I heard downtown that you had caught the clap," Tom said.

"How in the world could I have caught the clap?" asked the sick man.

Tom reached up, pulled the sheet away from his brother's body, and surveyed the situation. "Well," he said. "You may not have the clap, but you've got the worst case of the wilt I ever saw!"

One of our favorite Cheraw ladies had a baby, her first. When the infant was still quite young, she decided a beautiful child like hers should not be kept out of sight from an adoring public. She determined to take a stroll downtown, with baby in a carriage, to let people see how wonderfully God had blessed her. She entered many shops downtown where she had friends, and they oohed and aahed over the baby, who was indeed a handsome specimen. Then she entered the hardware store, where she had many friends. Hiney came up to greet her and bent over to examine the beautiful child. "Ugliest baby I ever saw in my life," he pronounced. Shocked and not understanding, she cut short her promenade and returned home. She hadn't been there fifteen minutes before her doorbell rang. She opened the door and found Miss Martha, the wife, standing there with a basket of tomatoes. "Hiney called and told me to get over here and mend some fences," she explained. "You didn't know it, but he says that about all new babies."

A young boy about to enter high school had been hearing horror stories about taking Latin the next year, so he talked to his mother.

"Mom, I don't think I'll take Latin next year."

"Why not, Son?"

"I ain't perfect in English yet."

Author's note: People are fun to watch, and they say funny things, too.